Original title:

Yondered Planks Beneath the Phoenix Tub

Author: Aron Pilviste

ISBN HARDBACK: 978-1-80562-305-2

ISBN PAPERBACK: 978-1-80563-826-1

Dreamscapes Found in Grainy Abodes

In corners dim, where shadows creep,
A tapestry of dreams does seep.
Whispers soft, like feathered sighs,
Nestle warmly, while daylight flies.

Upon the threads of silver light,
Minds wander gently into night.
In grainy textures, tales unwind,
Unspooling secrets left behind.

The flicker of a candle's glow,
Guides lost spirits, soft and slow.
From corners hidden, echoes call,
Of laughter mingled in the hall.

A dance of dust in beams of sun,
Where ancient stories still are spun.
In every knot, a memory found,
In grainy abodes, we are unbound.

Awakening the Spirit Through Timeless Flow

Upon the river, silent streams,
Awaken hearts from slumbered dreams.
The water speaks in gentle sighs,
Reflecting truths from starry skies.

A timeless flow that bids us wake,
Where every ripple holds a stake.
In currents deep, our spirits soar,
Awakening desires, evermore.

Whispers of the winds caress,
Each moment draped in tenderness.
Through ancient woods, the spirit trails,
A calling soft that never fails.

In dancing leaves, the stories blend,
Each turn of tide, a faithful friend.
Awakening echoes in the deep,
Where waters promise solace, sleep.

Ashen Hues Above the Sheltered Basin

In twilight's grip, the colors fade,
Ashen hues in silence played.
Above the basin, shadows loom,
A soft reminder of the gloom.

The stars, like embers, twinkle low,
In the embrace of night's soft flow.
Beneath the veil of cosmic glow,
The dreams of time begin to show.

In whispered winds, the tales unfurl,
Of distant lands, and ocean's swirl.
Each ashen hue, a story spun,
Held tight beneath the mourning sun.

Yet in this calm, a promise lies,
Renewal found beneath dark skies.
In every shadow, hope remains,
Ashen hues with golden veins.

Selves Transformed in Fiery Trials

Through trials fierce, the spirit bends,
In flames of change, a journey ends.
Emerging bright from ashen climes,
We rise anew in fiery rhymes.

With every test, the heart prevails,
In forged resolve, where courage sails.
Each scar a badge of battles fought,
In trials' grasp, true strength is sought.

From embers cold, a phoenix sings,
In fiery trials, new life springs.
Through cleansing heat, we cast away,
The shadows that would lead astray.

Transformed by fire, we come alive,
In faded ashes, hopes revive.
From trials steeped, we find our place,
In every flame, a spark of grace.

Driftwood Melodies of the Ancients

In whispers of the trees, tales unfold,
Of ancient travelers, brave and bold.
Driftwood dances in the gentle stream,
Carrying echoes of a lost dream.

Moonlight bathes the shore in silver light,
As shadows play in the stillness of night.
The waves chant ballads of years gone by,
Beneath a star-studded, vast sky.

Each piece of wood, a story to tell,
Of mariners' fates and their journeys' swell.
Nature's canvas, painted with time,
In driftwood's grip, emotions climb.

Listen closely, the melodies call,
A haunting reminder that we're all small.
With every crash, the seas do remind,
Of the ties that forever bind.

So gather around, let the stories flow,
Of driftwood and dreams, where ancients go.
In the heart of the forest and deep in the tide,
Lie the whispers of secrets, the worlds collide.

Awakening in Sunken Embers

Within the ash, a flicker lies,
A spark of hope 'neath smoky skies.
The scent of charcoal clings to the air,
Whispering tales of those who dare.

From the shadows, shadows rise,
Stretching towards the ancient skies.
Resilient flames, they dance in glee,
Awakening what's meant to be.

In the silence, hearts can hear,
The crackling music drawing near.
Resurrected dreams begin to glow,
In sunken embers, love will flow.

With every spark, the past ignites,
Illuminating darkened nights.
Fading whispers, yet ever bright,
Guide the lost with their tender light.

So gather 'round, let legends soar,
In this fire, we are evermore.
From ashes, we rise; we claim our fate,
In sunken embers, we await.

Heartbeats Beneath the Burning Surface

Heartbeats echo in the dark, deep wells,
Where secrets linger and time dwells.
Beneath the surface, a pulse remains,
A river of fire, igniting chains.

Dreams drift softly on the current's flow,
In hues of amber, they ebb and glow.
The burning essence of tales untold,
Wrapped in the warmth of spirits bold.

In hidden depths, a soft sigh flows,
Resilience blooms as the darkness grows.
Life unyielding, like a flame's soft song,
In the quiet depths, where we belong.

Each heartbeat tells of triumph's thrill,
Of souls entwined with unbreakable will.
Together they dance, beneath the flame,
Whispering softly each cherished name.

Bound by the rhythm, hearts beat as one,
A tapestry spun 'neath moon and sun.
Through the fire's embrace, we shall dive,
For heartbeats beneath are truly alive.

The Planks of Forgotten Journeys

Old planks whisper of journeys past,
Of ships that sailed, their die was cast.
Each knot and grain tells stories of old,
Of mariners brave, their courage bold.

Through storms they sailed, across the tide,
With laughter shared and fears defied.
In every crack, a memory hides,
Of love and loss, of turbulent rides.

Time wraps round like the ocean's embrace,
In the planks lie faces, each a trace.
Forgotten tales rise with the sun,
A voyage begun, its mark undone.

How many dreams were lost at sea?
What secrets wait for you and me?
In the wood's embrace, our fates entwined,
In forgotten journeys, hope we'll find.

So take a step on this weathered deck,
And feel the stories that life will sketch.
In planks of old, our lives renew,
For every journey begins anew.

Wings of Embered Reflections

In twilight's glow, the shadows play,
With whispers soft, they lead astray.
Beneath the stars, a secret flame,
Burns bright with hope, yet speaks thy name.

The echoes sigh in winds that weave,
A tapestry of dreams we believe.
Each flicker casts a spell so dear,
While hearts entwined dispel the fear.

From crumbled stones to skies of gold,
The tales of old are softly told.
In flickered light, our journeys stream,
On wings of ember, they dare to dream.

Each moment shared, a fleeting glance,
We dance on air in timeless chance.
The nightingale sings a sweet refrained,
As shadows blend where love remains.

So gather close, dear souls of light,
For in this bond, we find our flight.
Embered wings, let spirits rise,
In whispered dreams beneath the skies.

Sunlit Dreams on Weathered Wood

Upon the porch, the sunlight beams,
Through weathered wood, it finds our dreams.
Each splinter tells a tale of yore,
As time drips slow, forevermore.

The laughter mingles in the air,
With memories that linger there.
A gentle breeze, a soft embrace,
In sunlit moments, love finds its place.

With every tear the wood has shed,
A story of the life we've led.
In golden hues, our hearts align,
As shadows dance in sweet divine.

Around the table, tales unfold,
Of dreams exchanged, of love retold.
The sun dips low, our hearts will soar,
On weathered wood, we dream once more.

So raise a glass to time and trust,
In golden rays, we find our lust.
For sunlit dreams and weathered wood,
Remind us of this life we could.

Whispers of Dreams in the Oasis

In desert sands, where silence reigns,
The whispers call through hot refrains.
Beneath the palms, a secret lies,
In stillness, hear the softest sighs.

The moon will rise with gentle grace,
Reflecting dreams in this vast space.
A crystal brook, where shadows play,
In whispers soft, it leads the way.

In warm embrace of night's caress,
We wander forth to seek, to bless.
For in the oasis, hearts unfold,
Where every story is retold.

With every star, a promise glows,
Of paths unknown where magic flows.
In dreams, we find the truth concealed,
As desert winds our hearts have healed.

So let us chase the whispers near,
Through sands of time, let's shed our fear.
In dreams of love within this space,
We'll find our home, our timeless place.

Ascent of the Fiery Bird

In dawn's embrace, the phoenix wakes,
With embered heart, the silence breaks.
With wings of flame, it soars anew,
A dance of light in skies of blue.

Through trials faced, it learns to rise,
Each fleeting moment, wise and wise.
The ashes whisper tales of yore,
As fiery souls ignite the shore.

With every beat, the world transforms,
A symphony that love adorns.
With open heart, the flames ignite,
In unity, they pierce the night.

So let the flames soar high and free,
For in their light, we find the key.
To dreams fulfilled and hope reborn,
In fiery flight, a new world's dawn.

Embrace the fire, let spirits soar,
In every heart, the wild roar.
For life's ascent, a vibrant blaze,
Ascent of the bird, through endless days.

Searing Reflections on Echoing Waters

In the depths, the shadows sway,
Mirrors gleam, where secrets play.
Ripples dance on the moonlit skin,
Whispers dwell where dreams begin.

Thoughts unfurl beneath the haze,
Starlit glimmers set ablaze.
In each wave, a tale untold,
Of brave hearts and spirits bold.

The waters churn, time's gentle quill,
Inscribing fates with silent thrill.
In echoes deep, the laughter lies,
Beneath the watchful, velvet skies.

Every droplet holds a glance,
Lost in time, a fleeting chance.
With every pulse, a heartbeats' plea,
To uncover what's yet to see.

In searing light, reflections seep,
Through history's hands, they slowly creep.
A tapestry, woven with care,
Binding memories in the air.

In the Wake of Fiery Spirits

Flames arise with vibrant grace,
In their glow, we find our place.
Echoes cackle in the night,
Guiding souls beyond our sight.

Flickering shadows dance with glee,
Woven tales of mystery.
Every ember, a whispered name,
Fueling hopes that flicker and flame.

The night is rich, a tapestry,
Threads of magic, wild and free.
With every crackle, sparks take flight,
In the wake of fiery light.

Spirits soar on wings of fire,
In their blaze, we find our desire.
Weaving dreams beyond the veil,
In whispers soft, their truths unveil.

From ashes rise, our hearts take wing,
To the chorus of the spirits sing.
In the wake, we chase the morn,
Reborn from night, forever sworn.

Charred Lines of the Past

In the gloom, shadows are cast,
Etched in time, the marks of past.
Beneath the ash, the stories rest,
In charred lines, we seek the best.

Ghostly echoes softly sigh,
Of whispered dreams that learned to fly.
With trembling hands, we touch the flame,
To rekindle hopes that still remain.

Each scar a tale of lessons learned,
Through trials faced, our spirits burned.
In ember's glow, we find our thread,
To weave anew what once we bled.

From darkness borne, we rise again,
In charred lines, through loss and pain.
With every breath, we stitch the seams,
Binding together our weary dreams.

The past a canvas, colors blend,
In smoky hues, we make amends.
Through charred remains, our truths are found,
In the silence, hope unbound.

Layers of Ash and Liquid Light

Underneath the quiet night,
Layers blend, in ash and light.
With every breath, a tale unfolds,
Of whispered dreams and heartbeats bold.

Liquid light moves through the air,
With every flicker, a gentle care.
Ashen memories swirl around,
In this place where thoughts are found.

Each shadow carries tales untold,
Of restless souls, of hearts of gold.
Beneath the surface, stories sleep,
In layers deep, their secrets keep.

Radiance glows as night takes flight,
In harmony of ash and light.
Through every layer, new worlds arise,
Each shining moment never dies.

With courage fierce, we face the dawn,
As daylight stirs, the night is drawn.
In layers woven, hope takes flight,
Through ashes bright, we chase the light.

Glints of Ash on a Bright Horizon

In twilight's glow, the embers spark,
Reflecting dreams in shadows dark.
With every flicker, hopes arise,
To chase the stars in velvet skies.

A journey starts where ashes lay,
With whispers of a brand-new day.
The winds carry tales of old,
Of battles fought and hearts of gold.

Though storms may rage and tempests swell,
A light persists, a magic spell.
For in the ruins, seeds are sown,
From glints of ash, new worlds are grown.

So raise your gaze to distant heights,
Embrace the dawn, defy the nights.
With every step, let spirits soar,
Towards bright horizons, evermore.

Resurgence Along the Worn Path

Along the path of weary feet,
Where tales of time and seasons meet.
The echoes of the past resound,
In every stone that's kiss'd the ground.

With every step, a lesson learned,
Through twists of fate, the heart has turned.
The will to rise, to seek, to find,
Brings light anew to weary minds.

Beneath the leaves, old secrets hide,
While flowers bloom with spring's soft tide.
Yet through the thorns and tangled vines,
Resilience whispered, hope aligns.

So as you walk, let shadows fade,
In every heartbeat, dreams are made.
For journeys weave a tapestry,
In every step, your spirit's free.

Where Shadows Dance with Flames

In the heart of night, where shadows play,
A fire ignites, chasing night away.
Lurking in corners, whispers creep,
While secrets in the darkness sleep.

The flickering light calls forth the brave,
To face the fears that dark hearts pave.
With every spark, a courage grows,
In shadows' dance, the true heart shows.

Yet shadows linger, secrets hide,
In the flicker, hope and fear collide.
For every flame that boldly leaps,
A flicker deep in silence keeps.

So join the dance, embrace the night,
For in the dark, we find our light.
Together we rise, in flames we trust,
Where shadows fall, our spirits lust.

The Whispering Tides of Transformation

The ocean's breath, a gentle muse,
In waves of change, old souls infuse.
With every tide that swells and falls,
A promise sings, a siren calls.

As grains of sand shift with the flow,
New dreams arise, old ones let go.
The rhythm sways like an ancient dance,
In every crest, a fleeting chance.

Beneath the moon, reflections gleam,
Time reshapes fate, like a lucid dream.
With whispered secrets in the foam,
The tides bring forth a brand-new home.

So let the currents guide your way,
Embrace the change, come what may.
For in the ebb, the flow unfolds,
A tale of life in waves retold.

Emergence from Below the Faded Wood

From shadows deep where secrets lie,
Roots entwined with dreams gone by.
A whispered tale in twilight's breath,
Awakens life, defying death.

Through tangled vines, a glimmer shines,
A surge of hope, where darkness whines.
Beneath the bark, the stories swell,
Of magic lost, yet here to dwell.

Each leaf a memory, soft and bright,
Guiding souls through the night.
The forest sings of times long past,
In every breeze, a spell cast.

With every chirp, the dawn breaks clear,
Courage blooms, chasing fear.
In the heart of wood, old spirits wake,
Uniting paths, and lives they take.

So venture forth, both bold and free,
Embrace the path that's meant to be.
From faded wood, a new refrain,
A world reborn, from love and pain.

Dreams of the Resilient Heart

In whispered tones, the heart beats strong,
A melody that feels like home.
Through trials faced, in shadows cast,
Hope ignites and fears are past.

As night descends with stars aglow,
Resilience grows, a steady flow.
Each tear a pearl, each scar a line,
In pain, we find what's pure and fine.

The dreams we weave, both bold and bright,
Illuminate our darkest night.
With courage stitched in every seam,
We chase the echoes of our dream.

So lift your gaze to skies anew,
With every dawn, the world breaks through.
For in the heart, where hope resides,
True strength is found, and joy abides.

The road may twist, the path unclear,
But trust the heart, let go of fear.
With dreams as wings, we rise and soar,
To reach the stars forevermore.

Burnished Whispers of Soft Waters

In rippling grace, the waters speak,
Of hidden tales, both strong and meek.
Each ripple mirrors the soulful night,
Illuming dreams in soft moonlight.

The breeze carries whispers sweet and low,
Where dreams drift gently, like falling snow.
Reflecting worlds in crystal glow,
In every wave, a story flows.

With every current, secrets twine,
In silver depths where spirits shine.
Surrendered hopes, like petals drift,
The heart finds peace, a tender gift.

So let the waters guide your way,
Beneath the sky, a brighter day.
In nature's flow, find your release,
Where chaos ceases, and hearts find peace.

For in these streams, where soft winds blow,
Life's subtle melody will grow.
With burnished whispers, pure and clear,
Embrace the silence, hold it near.

The Resilient Path of Time

Along the path where shadows play,
Time coils back, then slips away.
In every step, a lesson learned,
Through winding trails, frail hearts burned.

With patience carved in stone and clay,
The seasons shift, then fade and sway.
From every autumn's crisp embrace,
Springs forth the strength, a gentle grace.

For moments fleeting, quick as light,
Hold precious dreams with all your might.
The echoes linger, soft yet clear,
In whispered tales, let go of fear.

In laughter's ring and sorrow's song,
The paths we tread, so wide, so long.
Each twist and turn, a story spun,
A dance of shadows, bright as sun.

So walk with courage, stones align,
Embrace the heart, let visions shine.
For time may bend, but never break,
The resilient souls, we rise, we wake.

The Alchemist's Dream of Rebirth

In shadows deep, secrets grow,
The heart of gold in a flickering glow.
With whispers of hope and embers bright,
The alchemist dreams in the still of night.

From ashes past, a potion flows,
Transforming life, as the river knows.
Through trials faced, and fears overcome,
New beginnings rise, a life reborn.

The spiraled paths of fate entwine,
In every drop, a tale divine.
A silver spark ignites the air,
In this rich brew, the world laid bare.

With heart and wand, the journey starts,
To craft a future with fiery arts.
An ancient lore, a timeless scheme,
The alchemist's dream, to break the seam.

So seek the wisdom in a child's gaze,
In laughter sweet, and simple praise.
For in their eyes, magic lives on,
A spark of hope, from dusk till dawn.

Refracted Glory in Water's Warm Embrace

In liquid mirrors, stories dance,
A world unveiled through chance and glance.
With every ripple, colors blend,
In water's warmth, the dreams ascend.

The sunbeams kiss the surface clear,
With rainbows woven, bright and sheer.
Each drop a prism, life's embrace,
Reflected beauty in gentle grace.

Amidst the waves, a whisper sings,
Of ancient lore and hidden things.
A saga spun from water's thread,
Echoes of glories long since fled.

As currents shift, a tale unfolds,
In shimmering depths, the heart beholds.
A tapestry of twilight hues,
In water's arms, the soul renews.

Herein lies magic, pure and rare,
In every splash, a breath of air.
Refracted glory, twilight's song,
In water's warmth, where dreams belong.

The Spirit's Ascent from Liquid Dreams

Beneath the waves, the whispers swell,
In liquid dreams, the spirits dwell.
From shadowed depths, they rise to light,
In twinkling glimmers, a dance of flight.

With every tide, a heartbeat flows,
In liquid realms where freedom grows.
The currents pulse with ancient grace,
A silver thread in time and space.

As bubbles burst, a laughter sounds,
In harmony with nature's rounds.
The spirit's song, a mighty breeze,
In liquid dreams, the heart finds ease.

In soaring arcs, the waters part,
The essence blooms, an artist's heart.
With every drop, the cosmos hums,
And from the depths, the spirit comes.

So dive into the depths of night,
Embrace the wonder, the pure delight.
For liquid dreams are where we soar,
A spirit's ascent forevermore.

Echoing Ashes in Twilight

As twilight falls, the past awakes,
In whispered winds, the memory stakes.
Each ember glows with tales untold,
Echoing ashes, a life of gold.

The shadows stretch across the land,
In fading light, we take a stand.
For every spark, a journey starts,
And echoes linger in tender hearts.

Through ghostly hues, the moments play,
Where laughter danced, now shadows sway.
In every sigh, a flicker stays,
In twilight's calm, the spirit sways.

With fallen leaves, the stories spin,
Of love and loss, where dreams begin.
In quiet spaces, the heart keeps score,
Echoing ashes, forevermore.

So weave your memories into the night,
As twilight holds us, soft and light.
For in the echoes, a truth resides,
In ashes whispered, the heart confides.

The Lament of the Phoenix Plume

In twilight's grasp, the plume does weep,
For memories lost in the ashes deep.
Once vibrant wings in the sun's embrace,
Now mere whispers in a shadowed space.

Yet in sorrow, sparks ignite,
A dance with fate, a flickering light.
From sorrow's cradle, a fire shall rise,
In each farewell, a new sunrise.

In flames of red, the heart shall soar,
Through trials faced on the ancient floor.
With every tear, a story spun,
The phoenix knows its race is run.

But hope is woven in petals bright,
In embered dreams that pierce the night.
For every end begins anew,
The cycle breathes where sky meets blue.

Celestial Reflections on a Fiery Floor

Beneath a sky with stars aglow,
A floor of embers begins to show.
Their dance reflects in fiery hues,
While echoes linger of ancient truths.

The cosmos spins, a grand ballet,
As flames in whispers softly play.
Each flicker writes the tales of old,
Of courage forged and hearts turned bold.

In radiant warmth, shadows flee,
Revealing worlds yet to be.
Each spark a wish, a hopeful plea,
In the universe's endless sea.

With every glow, a chance reborn,
On fiery floors where dreams adorn.
Celestial songs in night's embrace,
Shine through darkness, a sacred space.

Resilience of the Embered Heart

In deepest night, when silence reigns,
The embered heart, it breaks its chains.
From ashes cold, a warmth ascends,
A tale of strength where light transcends.

With every trial, the spirit bends,
Yet through each crack, the fire mends.
Resilience holds the fiercest will,
A flicker's dance on the edge of thrill.

The sparks of hope ignite the dark,
In shadows cast, it leaves a mark.
With every beat, a quiet grace,
The embered heart finds its place.

Though storms may rage and winds may howl,
It stands steadfast, fierce as an owl.
From embers born of a heart once torn,
A new dawn waits, a world reborn.

The Dance of Fire and Spirit

In the hush of dusk, the fire twirls,
Spirit and flame, in a dance that swirls.
With every flicker, a story unfolds,
Whispers of magic, the night beholds.

They leap and spin in a vibrant rhyme,
Echoing legends lost in time.
A rhythm beats in every spark,
In the surge of light, they leave their mark.

With passion fierce, the flames invite,
To join their waltz beneath the night.
In every turn, the shadows sway,
As spirits rise to join the fray.

Together they weave a tapestry bright,
In the heart of darkness, anointing light.
In the dance of fire, a truth shall gleam,
A fiery bond, igniting dream.

Beneath the Surface of Dreams Afloat

In silence deep, the dreams do weave,
Forgotten tales, where wishes cleave.
Beneath the waves, in twilight's hold,
The secrets of the heart unfold.

With colors bright that softly glow,
They dance like whispers, sweet and low.
A world that glimmers, tender, shy,
Where moments sparkle, time drifts by.

Here, shadows play with moonlit grace,
Each flicker hides a warm embrace.
In gentle sway of dreams afloat,
A heart can soar, a spirit float.

Yet as the dawn brings forth its light,
The dreams take flight, hidden from sight.
A fragile thread, they twine and spin,
Awakening the soul within.

Harmonics of Ash and Dust

In twilight's breath, the embers sigh,
As echoes linger, soft and dry.
From ashes cold, a symphony wakes,
Of moments lost, of shadowed stakes.

The whispers of the past embrace,
Each note a memory, each trace.
In dust we find the stories told,
Of hearts entwined, both shy and bold.

With every flicker, tales arise,
Of love and loss, beneath dark skies.
The harmony of life laid bare,
In rhythm lost, yet always there.

Like fleeting dreams, the sounds will fade,
Yet in the silence, memories played.
Of ashes sprinkled on the ground,
The echoes of the lost resound.

The Serpent's Embrace of the Sun

In golden light, the serpent coils,
Around the warmth where daylight spoils.
With scales that shimmer, dark and bright,
It weaves a dance, a wondrous sight.

The sun, a flame, gives life anew,
In swirls of heat, a vibrant hue.
They twine and twist, a sacred bond,
Between the light and shadows fond.

In whispers soft, the stories grow,
Of ancient myths, where secrets flow.
In every turn, the truth concealed,
An ardent heart forever healed.

Together bound in time's embrace,
They offer warmth, they offer grace.
From serpent's touch to sun's pure glow,
A partnership the ages know.

Flights of Fancy Amidst Charred Shadows

In realms of ash, where dreams once soared,
The spirit whispers, never bored.
Among the charred and twisted trees,
The flight of fancies floats on breeze.

Through shadows dark, the wings will glide,
With hopes that flicker, hearts won't hide.
In every flutter, tales unfold,
Of brave hearts bold, and dreams retold.

The embers speak in colors bright,
Of battles fought and won by night.
For in the dusk, new worlds take flight,
And fancy reigns over the fright.

So let the shadows blend and bend,
For in their depths, our dreams ascend.
With every pulse, imagination thrives,
In flights of fancy, the heart revives.

Forgotten Tales from the Water's Edge

Whispers echo in the fading light,
Where secrets rest beneath the tide.
Old tales cling to the roots of dreams,
In twilight's glow, their truths reside.

Beneath the waves, the echoes stir,
Of voices lost to sands of time.
Each ripple carries hope and fear,
In the shimmer, old loves chime.

The moonlit path where shadows dance,
Remembers every silent song.
Each drop of dew, a tale unspooled,
Where ancient hearts forever long.

The evening breeze begins to tell,
Of ships that sailed to distant shores.
Their memories wrapped in salty mist,
Brought back by winds and whispered oars.

In the dark depths, the stories weave,
Of fortune lost and battles fought.
The water's edge holds all our dreams,
In currents where the past is caught.

Symphony of Heat and Embers

Where firelight dances with the night,
A symphony of warmth unfolds.
The embers whisper ancient tales,
In crackling voices, brave and bold.

The flames leap high with joy and pain,
Their flickers chase the shadows near.
In every spark, a memory lives,
Burning bright through strands of fear.

Through smoky air, the laughter swells,
Of friendships forged 'neath starry skies.
Each glowing ember, a captured wish,
In the night's embrace, forever flies.

With every log that slowly wanes,
The warmth of hearts begins to blend.
A cycle spins, a silent vow,
To cherish all that time would send.

So gather close, let stories flow,
In this snug haven of pure light.
Amidst the heat, the embers sing,
A timeless hymn that warms the night.

Visions Carved in Resilient Grain

In the forest deep, where silence reigns,
Trees stand tall, their limbs embrace.
Each ring a story, a whisper shared,
Etched in wood, time's trace of grace.

The wind carries songs of ages past,
Through branches swaying in gentle rhythm.
Each rustle wraps a tale anew,
In nature's heart, they find their prism.

Beneath the bark, a world concealed,
In shadows soft, the life goes on.
Mighty roots stretch through the earth,
In silence deep, they find their song.

As seasons turn, their wisdom grows,
With every storm, they bend, not break.
Resilient beings in light and dark,
In whispered winds, their futures wake.

So heed the trees and all they tell,
Of trials met with steadfast grace.
For strength is carved in the grain of love,
In every heart, a sacred place.

Melodies Beneath the Feathered Gleam

In the dawn's light, where feathers glow,
Birdsong weaves a tender lace.
Each note a ripple through the air,
A joy that time cannot erase.

Beneath the boughs where shadows sway,
The melodies in whispers play.
They dance on breezes soft and clear,
As if the world begins to sway.

The fluttering wings in morning's grace,
Paint stories vivid in the sky.
With every call, they share their dreams,
In vibrant echoes, soaring high.

As sunlight warms the waking day,
The chorus swells, inviting all.
The symphony of life unfolds,
With every note, the heart recalls.

So linger here, let music flow,
In the feathered gleam of dawn's embrace.
For in each song, a world ignites,
With every flutter, a timeless grace.

The Wood's Secret Beneath Radiant Skies

In whispers soft, the branches sway,
A tale of old, where shadows play,
Beneath the leaves, a path is found,
Where ancient magic stirs the ground.

The squirrels dart through dappled light,
As sunlight spills, a golden sight,
An owl takes flight, her eyes so wise,
Guarding secrets 'neath the skies.

The mossy stones, with stories bold,
Of lovers lost and heroes told,
With every step, a heartbeat thrums,
In nature's heart, the silence hums.

A breeze that carries scents of pine,
Invites the soul to intertwine,
With whispered dreams, a gentle calm,
The wood's embrace, a soothing balm.

In twilight's glow, a hidden door,
To realms unknown, on woodland floor,
Where time stands still, and wishes grow,
Beneath the stars, the secrets flow.

Depths of Dreams Entwined with Fire

In the heart of night, the flames do dance,
Ember's glow, a fleeting chance,
To glimpse the dreams, both dark and bright,
Entwined in shadows, wrapped in light.

A flicker stirs, a secret told,
Of passions fierce, of love so bold,
These fiery hearts, they intertwine,
In depths of dreams, where souls align.

With every spark that pierces through,
A whisper calls, a promise true,
The warmth like magic, fierce yet kind,
In every flicker, hope we find.

A dance of light, it draws us near,
In flames we see what we hold dear,
Its gentle heat on faces bright,
Illuminates the depths of night.

As dawn approaches, embers fade,
Yet in the heart, the fire stayed,
A memory forged, forever bright,
In dreams entwined with endless light.

The Interlude of Spark and Water

When droplets fall, a gentle sound,
Amidst the silence, life is found,
The spark of joy, a fleeting gleam,
In puddles deep, we chase a dream.

A shimmer soft, like silver threads,
Weaving stories where laughter spreads,
In dancing streams, reflections gleam,
Of worlds entwined, of truth and dream.

As rivers flow and currents sway,
The sparks ignite a bright array,
In every splash, a heart ignites,
The union of two wild delights.

Oceans roar, yet gentle tides,
Harbor secrets where love abides,
In every wave, a spark takes flight,
An interlude of day and night.

When rain and sun embrace the earth,
A rainbow arcs, a symbol of worth,
In nature's dance, a joyful place,
The spark and water's warm embrace.

The Saga of Fiery Transitions

In twilight's haze, the embers glow,
As day surrenders to night's flow,
With every breath, a change unfolds,
A saga born, of tales retold.

A journey through the shifting sands,
Where time and fate weave tender strands,
In every turn, a lesson learned,
Through fiery trials, the heart is burned.

From ashes rise the dreams anew,
A phoenix fierce, with courage true,
In every flicker, a pathway shines,
The saga forged in fiery lines.

Amidst the flames, a song ascends,
Of love and loss, where hope transcends,
A bright horizon, a beckoning light,
In fiery transitions, the spirit's flight.

So hold the fire, let it inspire,
In every heart, an ancient fire,
For in the saga, we find our way,
Through fiery transitions, come what may.

Flames Cradled in Serene Depths

In shadows deep where whispers dwell,
A flicker glows, a secret spell.
Embers dance in gentle sway,
Cradled soft, the night turns gray.

The stillness holds a tempered breath,
A cradle forged from life and death.
Each spark a tale of hidden dreams,
In the deep, the fire gleams.

Beneath the water, stories weave,
A tapestry where none believe.
Yet in the dark, the flames ignite,
Illuminating fragile night.

The silent depths, they listen close,
To whispered thoughts, they dare to boast.
What lies beneath the quiet crest,
Can cradle flames and grant them rest.

In this embrace of dark and light,
The spirit soars beyond the night.
For in the blend of calm and fire,
We find the depths that rise higher.

The Wooden Path of Rebirth

Upon the path of ancient wood,
Where time stands still, and sorrow's good.
Each step a promise, fresh and new,
In every grain, the past shines through.

The branches stretch, their arms unfold,
In stories whispered, strong and bold.
With every footfall soft and bright,
We walk the woods, we find our light.

The tapestry of seasons change,
In hues of life, both sweet and strange.
From roots of sorrow, bloom the bright,
A dance of shadows and of light.

Beneath the canopy's embrace,
We find ourselves, a sacred place.
With every leaf that falls and sways,
We learn to rise through shadowed days.

As whispers blend with rustling leaves,
We gather strength from what deceives.
The wooden path, a thread of grace,
Leads forth to life, a new embrace.

Ashen Reflections in a Still Pool

In twilight's gaze, the waters lie,
A mirror holds the fading sky.
Among the ashes, memories swirl,
In ripples soft, the secrets unfurl.

Each token smoldered, left to drift,
Like dreams once bright, now held as gift.
In stillness deep, we take our chance,
To touch the past in fleeting dance.

The shadows flicker, whispers sing,
In quiet tones, the echoes cling.
While ashen forms begin to fade,
The pool reflects what time has made.

From pain and loss, a beauty grows,
In silent depths, the heart bestows.
A chance to see what once was real,
In stillness found, we learn to heal.

With every glance, the past takes flight,
In mirrored depths, we find our light.
For in the ashes, hope will bloom,
In still pools, dispelling gloom.

Phoenix Wings over Hallowed Wood

Through ancient trees the whispers soar,
In sacred groves, they seek for more.
With wings of flame and heart of gold,
The phoenix flies, a tale retold.

Beneath the boughs where shadows blend,
A promise made, a journey's end.
The spirit arcs, a fiery trace,
In hallowed woods, we find our place.

From ashes born, its flight begins,
A dance of hope, where life begins.
In vibrant hues, the sky ignites,
In every heart, the phoenix bites.

As night gives way to dawn's embrace,
We rise anew, a brighter grace.
With wings unfurled, we chase the light,
In hallowed wood, we take to flight.

The whispers call, the journey's long,
But in our hearts, we sing our song.
For with each beat, the fire thrives,
In phoenix wings, our spirit flies.

The Last Flight of the Embered Hope

In twilight's arms, a whisper flies,
A flicker bright in darkened skies.
Hope dances lightly, a fragile thing,
On wings of fire, it takes to spring.

Through gales of doubt, its shimmer glows,
A beacon born where shadows close.
It soars above the dismal gray,
Filling hearts with light, come what may.

Yet in the night, the ember fades,
A softness in the serenades.
But deep within, the spark resides,
A silent vow the soul abides.

So let the winds remember well,
The whispered dreams, the tales to tell.
Though tempests roar and sorrow's near,
The embered hope will persevere.

With every trial, a lesson gleaned,
In every heart, a fire dreamed.
A final flight, a fleeting glimpse,
Of destinies entwined in brilliant hymns.

Journey Through Glow and Shadow

Upon a path where shadows blend,
A tale begins that will not end.
With every step, a heartbeat shared,
The glow of light, a soul laid bare.

Whispers linger in the night,
A dance of dark, a spark of light.
Through tangled woods, the spirits sing,
In harmony around the spring.

Yet time slips past, as moonlight wanes,
In stillness deep, the journey gains.
Each twist and turn, a choice bestowed,
With every heartbeat, wisdom flowed.

The glow embraced, the shadows learned,
In unity, the heart discerned.
From dark to light, a thread interwoven,
In every soul, a path unspoken.

From dawn to dusk, the saga glows,
In every heart where courage grows.
A journey marked by love and grace,
Through glow and shadow, we find our place.

Resurgent Forces Beneath Stillness

In silence found beneath the earth,
A pulse awaits, a brewing birth.
Where roots entwine, a force concealed,
A power bold, yet unrevealed.

The winds may hush, the stars may wait,
Yet in the dark, they cultivate.
From ashes cold to skies anew,
A tempest brews, a vibrant hue.

Within the depths, the whispers rise,
In every heartbeat, life defies.
Awakening storms from slumber deep,
A promise made, a pact to keep.

The stillness breaks with fervent might,
As dreams ignite in blushing light.
The forces merge, a dance refined,
In every heart, the brave aligned.

Resurgent flames, a chorus swell,
In every heart, a tale to tell.
When stillness reigns, then know the truth,
The hidden strength of timeless youth.

The Space Between Cradle and Flame

In twilight's grasp, a cradle swings,
Embers warm with whispered dreams.
Between the hush and fire's embrace,
A delicate dance, a sacred space.

With every flicker, shadows play,
The heart's own light, a guiding ray.
In moments brief, where silence swells,
A tapestry of starlight dwells.

The cradle rocks with tender care,
While flames leap high, with laughter rare.
In every heartbeat, time suspends,
A fleeting gift that never ends.

The line between, a choice replete,
Where courage blooms, and spirits meet.
In every dusk, the dawn awaits,
A promise held, as fate creates.

So linger long in this embrace,
Between the cradle and the flame's grace.
For in the quiet, truths unfold,
A symphony of warmth, retold.

Secrets Harbored in the Quiet Depths

In the stillness of the night,
Whispers float on shadowed wings,
Veils that drape the hidden light,
Countless truths the darkness sings.

Beneath the surface, dreams decay,
Drowned in tales of sighs and fears,
Time slips through like grains of clay,
Etching memories through the years.

Lurking deep, the secrets crawl,
In caverns lined with ancient stone,
Echoes haunting every hall,
In silence, many truths are sown.

Veins of gold in murky shrouds,
Guardians of the stories told,
In shadows, destiny enshrouds,
The brave who seek the hearts of gold.

Let your soul dive into the fold,
Where whispered winds of past remain,
For hidden wonders still unfold,
In depths where only dreams can gain.

Echoes of Time Beneath the Waters

Beneath the waves, the past is caught,
In currents fierce, where shadows swirl,
Time's soft whispers, moments fraught,
In depths where ancient echoes twirl.

Ripples brush against the soul,
Cradling tales of what has been,
Each drop a story, a lost scroll,
Reflections murky, yet so keen.

Bubbles rise with laughter bright,
Underneath the sapphire dome,
Light dances from the depths of night,
A watery realm, a silent home.

Rustling sands with secrets keep,
For ages past, buried with care,
Nurtured dreams in silence sleep,
In liquid worlds, so deep and rare.

To dive is to embrace the call,
Where time stands still, and shadows grace,
For in the depths, we find it all—
A mirror of our fleeting trace.

The Nesting Cradle of the Ashen Flame

Within the heart of embers warm,
A cradle sways of ash and night,
It whispers softly 'neath the storm,
A beacon found in faded light.

Threads of smoke weave tales untold,
Of lives consumed and hopes set free,
In warmth, a language rich and bold,
The flame's embrace—eternity.

Feathers drift from heights unknown,
To nestle close in gathering winds,
Each flicker sings of seeds once sown,
In time's own garden, life begins.

The glow of hope on shadows cast,
Illuminates the paths we tread,
Through trials conquered, love amassed,
From ashes, beauty's gently fed.

So hold the flame, both tender and bright,
Let it guide through dark despair,
For in the heart of that warm light,
The nesting cradle waits and cares.

Resonance of Lost Flora

In corners where the wild things grow,
Whispers bloom in colors bold,
Petals painted by the flow,
Of memories, like tales retold.

Forgotten seeds from ages past,
Awake within the soil's embrace,
In shadows deep, they linger fast,
A dance of beauty, woven grace.

Where sunlight filters through the leaves,
And dew-kissed dreams unfold anew,
Nature's hand, the heart believes,
In silent hues that still pursue.

Echos of blooms that once were bright,
Now resting where few tread their way,
But still they whisper through the night,
In fragrant notes of joy and sway.

So heed the call of nature's song,
For in each petal lies a spark,
In lost flora, the roots belong,
Resonance found within the dark.

Shadows of Char upon Water's Edge

Beneath the twilight's gentle sway,
Shadows dance where whispers play.
Charred remnants of the fading light,
Secrets sowed in depths of night.

The water's edge reflects the skies,
Beneath the stars, a hidden guise.
Ripples tell of stories lost,
In the stillness, pain embossed.

Eclipsed by dreams of yesteryear,
Lingering hopes, a trace of fear.
Each wave carries a haunting song,
Of love and loss, and where we belong.

The breeze brings tales of ancient trees,
Whispers of hope, a gentle tease.
Shadows flicker like fleeting thoughts,
Echoing back what time forgot.

Yet in the char, the embers glow,
A chance for flight from depths below.
For every shadow holds its flame,
A promise made, a lover's name.

The Glade of Phoenix Echoes

In a glade where dreams ignite,
Phoenix rise in brilliant flight.
Echoes linger, soft and sweet,
Binding hearts where shadows meet.

Golden feathers in the air,
Whispers of a love laid bare.
Nature sings a timeless song,
In the glade where souls belong.

Beneath the boughs of ancient kin,
Hope resurges, fierce within.
Crimson petals on the ground,
Mark the places joy was found.

The sun dips low, the twilight glows,
In the silence, magic flows.
Every heartbeat, every sigh,
Breathes the promise to comply.

Resilient hearts, they rise anew,
Transforming pain to shining hue.
In the glade, forever bright,
A story spun in endless light.

Sooty Memories in a Liquid Mirror

In a mirror made of liquid glass,
Sooty memories softly pass.
Reflections speak of days long past,
Whispers of a love held fast.

Each droplet tells a woven tale,
Of winds that carried hope's sweet sail.
Fragments of laughter, echoes pure,
In this realm, the heart's allure.

Run fingers through the water's sheen,
Discover paths that might have been.
Sooty trails of bittersweet,
In the mirror, losses meet.

As twilight falls, the shadows creep,
Awakening the dreams we keep.
Liquid strokes define the scar,
Reminding us just who we are.

Yet from the depths, a light will rise,
Kindling hope in shadowed skies.
For every memory, dark or bright,
Shapes our journey to the light.

Kindled Stories along the Shimmering Bay

At the bay where whispers bloom,
Kindled stories chase the gloom.
Tales of sailors, lost and found,
Carried forth by waves profound.

Moonlight glistens on the tide,
Guiding hearts that seek to bide.
Seashell echoes call and yearn,
Every turn, a page to turn.

Footsteps pressed on sandy shores,
In the silence, adventure soars.
Rippling tales of beauty, grace,
In the bay's embrace, we trace.

Each flicker in the starry night,
Illuminates the heart's delight.
Laughter dances, spirits sway,
Along the edge of shimmering bay.

Yet in the calm, a tempest brews,
A story waits, the heart renews.
For every tide that ebbs or flows,
Kindled stories, love bestows.

Radiance Under the Churning Tide

Beneath the waves, a glow does lie,
Dancing lights as dark sails fly.
Secrets whispered, tides confess,
Life beneath in soft caress.

Moonlit beams through foamy crests,
A message penned by ocean's jest.
Nature's wisdom, old and wise,
Hides in depths with stars, it lies.

In currents wild, truth finds a path,
At sea's embrace, we feel its wrath.
Still, the heart knows when to swim,
In radiant dreams, we seek not dim.

Each crest, a tale of hopes anew,
Of wishes cast in morning dew.
Within the tide's unsteady sway,
Our spirits dance, and fears decay.

So when the storm begins to roar,
Remember light lies at the core.
In churning tides, we will abide,
And find our peace where dreams collide.

The Transcendent Plank Passage

A weathered path of wood and dreams,
Leads to places lost in beams.
Each step upon the ancient grain,
Whispers stories draped in rain.

The air is thick with magic's breath,
Where shadows linger still from death.
Yet hope resides in every crack,
A world awaits just round the back.

Here wanderers seek what lies beyond,
In every moment, tight and fond.
The plank extends to skies afire,
Where wishes soar and hearts aspire.

With courage stitched in threads of gold,
We cross the bridge that fate has told.
Hand in hand through veils of mist,
A future bright, not to be missed.

The journey calls, the echoes sing,
The world awaits, a wondrous thing.
Take the step, embrace the sway,
In every heart, our dreams hold sway.

Smoldering Dreams on Quiet Shores

Beside the waves, where sand does kiss,
Dreams linger low, like whispered bliss.
In twilight hues, the embers glow,
A tapestry of fading flow.

Each grain of sand, a memory pressed,
Of laughter shared and longed for rest.
Stars awaken in velvet skies,
While time drifts on, like soft goodbyes.

The night unfolds its velvet wings,
A melody of soft heartstrings.
Smoldering thoughts, like fireflies,
Twinkle softly, where magic lies.

On quiet shores, the past remains,
Wrapped in dreams, where love sustains.
In each heartbeat, a tale recites,
Of fleeting joy in gentle nights.

So linger here, where silence dwells,
In nighttime's womb, where wish compels.
For in this hush, our souls take flight,
On smoldering dreams through the night.

The Flames' Gentle Embrace

In twilight's glow, the embers dance,
A warming light in flickered trance.
They call to hearts with whispers sweet,
In flames' embrace, we find our beat.

Each spark a story, bright and bold,
In flickers warm, our dreams unfold.
With gentle hands, the fire does weave,
A tapestry that helps us believe.

Around the hearth, we gather near,
In laughter shared, we cast away fear.
The flames will guide us, night by night,
As shadows play in softest light.

So open your heart to the fire's song,
In comfort found, we all belong.
Through fleeting moments, joy does rise,
In flames' embrace, we reach for skies.

Let each warm glow ignite the dreams,
And fill our lives with hopeful beams.
For in this warmth, we find our way,
In the flames' embrace, we choose to stay.

Traces of the Celestial Voyage

Above the stars where dreams take flight,
Whispers swirl in the velvet night.
A tapestry woven by cosmic grace,
Guided by hope in this boundless space.

Each twinkle tells tales of realms unseen,
Of distant worlds and worlds between.
In silver ribbons, secrets glide,
Painting the skies where wonders bide.

The moon, a lantern in twilight's embrace,
Illuminates shadows, a gentle trace.
Hearts entwined in the astral dance,
Captured in moments of fleeting chance.

Across the expanse, old stories sigh,
Where stardust beings learn to fly.
Their laughter echoes, a soft refrain,
Binding us all with joy and pain.

In the hush between night's quiet song,
Our spirits find where they belong.
For in the heavens, we discover the key,
Unraveling threads of eternity.

Gleams of Forgotten Echoes

In the heart of woods where memories lie,
The wind carries whispers, a soft goodbye.
Echoes of laughter, lost in the trees,
Dance with the shadows and drift with the breeze.

Beneath the boughs where time stands still,
Gentle reminders of fate and will.
Each leaf that falls bears witness to dreams,
Caught in the sunlight, or so it seems.

From forgotten paths where wanderers tread,
To the secret glades where adventures spread.
The pulse beneath nature's tender dome,
Calls out to souls who once made it home.

Stories unfold in each rustling sound,
As ancient echoes reach from the ground.
Mysteries pulse in the fading light,
Promises whispered through day and night.

So linger a moment, heed the call,
For echoes of past do not fade at all.
They shimmer with magic, elusive and bright,
In the hearts of those seeking the light.

Reverberations of the Phoenix Soul

From ashes that whisper of battles won,
A phoenix rises with the break of dawn.
In fiery hues, it takes to the skies,
Crafting new futures with radiant cries.

The flames that danced through the night's embrace,
Transform the darkness with tender grace.
In every heartbeat, a story ignites,
Of courage reborn in the fiercest fights.

With wings unfurled, in a glorious arc,
It soars through the heavens, igniting the spark.
A melody stirring, alive in the air,
A testament bright to resilience and care.

In the warmth of its glow, the world finds hope,
As hearts once shattered learn how to cope.
Through trials and tempests, it rises again,
Promising light after sorrow and pain.

So let your spirit be touched by this flame,
Embrace the journey, forget all the shame.
For in every ending, a new tale is spun,
A hymn for the brave, forever begun.

Shoreline of Embered Memories

Where waves meet the sand and secrets reside,
Embers of memories linger and glide.
The ocean's soft murmur, a lullaby sweet,
Calls forth the past where time feels complete.

In twilight's embrace, the stars gleam bright,
Drawing out whispers from day into night.
Footprints of lovers washed by the tide,
Echo the laughter of hearts open wide.

With every wave, a story unfolds,
Of dreams once woven and whispers bold.
Shells cradle moments as treasures to keep,
Guarding the secrets the sea dares to weep.

As the sun dips low, the horizon glows,
Painting the canvas where the soft wind blows.
Each flicker of firelight, a spark of the past,
Guiding our hearts to where shadows are cast.

So gather your stories upon the shore,
Let the tides carry them forevermore.
For in the embers, we find the divine,
A shoreline of memories, forever entwined.

Mornings Forged in Glistening Heat

The sun awakes, a fiery blaze,
Casting shadows through the trees.
Golden rays dance in a haze,
Whispering secrets on the breeze.

Birds sing loud their morning tune,
Each note a spark in the air.
Nature's canvas glows at noon,
With colors vibrant, bright, and rare.

The world stirs from its night-time peace,
As laughter mingles with the light.
Soft petals bloom, their beauty lease,
Inviting all to take in sight.

Heat envelops like a warm embrace,
In this realm where time flows slow.
Every moment holds a trace,
Of magic only mornings know.

So pause and breathe this gift of day,
With every ray, let worries cease.
In glistening heat, let heart hold sway,
And find your center in the peace.

The Harmony of Soot and Serenity

In the twilight's dusky glow,
Smoke curls like a whispered tale.
Gentle echoes of long ago,
Humble scents of evening veil.

The city sleeps, adorned in grime,
Yet beauty thrives in shadows cast.
In soot and silent, soft sublime,
The harmonious moments last.

Beneath the grime, a heartbeat breathes,
Soft sighs escape the city's soul.
In every crack, a secret weaves,
While whispers linger, softly whole.

From every alley, stories wake,
Of laughter, tears, and love's embrace.
In this canvas, dreams we stake,
Beneath the soot, we find our place.

So cherish moments, dark and light,
For harmony lies unconfined.
In soot and peace, the world's delight,
Is found in the heart, intertwined.

Cascade of Fireflies in Dusk's Embrace

As daylight fades, the dusk arrives,
A symphony of twinkling glow.
Fireflies dance, like whispered lives,
In gentle waves, they ebb and flow.

Their lanterns flick, a fleeting spark,
Chasing shadows across the green.
In twilight's breath, they weave their arc,
Painting night with a charm unseen.

Each flicker tells a tale of night,
Of dreams and secrets held so dear.
In this cascade of soft light bright,
The world transforms, its magic clear.

Beneath the stars, a dance unfolds,
Nature's rhythm, free and grand.
In night's caress, a story told,
In fireflies' waltz, we understand.

So watch them play, in awe abide,
As dusk embraces every hue.
In this moment, hearts collide,
With every spark, a world anew.

The Tale Beneath the Darkened Waters

In depths unknown, where shadows dwell,
A story waits, both dark and deep.
Beneath the ripples, secrets swell,
In liquid silence, dreams do weep.

The currents whisper ancient lore,
Of spirits lost, of ships long gone.
In every wave, a haunting roar,
A symphony of dusk and dawn.

Reflections tell of loves once spun,
And battles fought with fierce embrace.
In the stillness, time's just begun,
To weave its threads, a mystic lace.

So listen close, to stories pooled,
In darkened waters, veiled and pure.
Each tide, a tale of fate that ruled,
In these depths, hearts seek their cure.

For not all journeys end in light,
Some linger on where waters speak.
In myth and tide, our hopes ignite,
As we uncover what we seek.

Glimpses of Infinity Through Embered Eyes

In the twilight, secrets gleam,
Stars whisper tales of forgotten dreams,
Embers dance in the night so wide,
As shadows unfold where mysteries hide.

Glimmers of truth amidst the haze,
Time swirls gently in a cosmic maze,
Through embered eyes, the worlds ignite,
Awakening wonders that take to flight.

Every flicker, a story told,
Threads of fate woven, bright and bold,
In the silence, echoes of the past,
Fleeting moments that forever last.

In the glow, the fabric bends,
Boundless visions, where dreaming ends,
Through the flames, we chase the light,
Illuminated by the kiss of night.

Beyond the ashes, a new dawn breaks,
Wisdom flows like the softest lakes,
Infinity whispers through embered sighs,
Unveiling wonders through ancient guise.

The Cauldron of Reinvention

In shadows deep, where secrets brew,
Curiosities dance in misty hue,
A cauldron simmers with dreams reborn,
Stirring magic at the break of dawn.

Fragments of old, in the potion swirl,
The past embraces as futures unfurl,
Each ingredient a tale to be spun,
Underneath stars, the journey's begun.

Transformation whispers in every blend,
Crafting new paths where lost dreams mend,
With a flick of the wrist, worlds change form,
In the heart of chaos, a calm is born.

From ashes and ruins, miracles rise,
In the bubbling depths, one learns to fly,
The cauldron hums with the pulse of time,
Reinvention blooms in rhythm and rhyme.

So gather your hopes, a potion to share,
In the alchemist's embrace, let go of despair,
Together we'll forge what was once been,
In the cauldron of life, we are forever seen.

Waves of Regeneration Underneath

Beneath the surface, the waters sing,
Rippling echoes of what dreams bring,
Waves of change, a gentle flow,
Regenerating all that we know.

In the depths, old whispers call,
The cycle spins, yet we stand tall,
Life reclaims what storms have tossed,
In the purity found, we find what's not lost.

With each tide, a lesson learned,
From shadows, light is brightly earned,
Beneath the waves, our spirits play,
Drifting freely, come what may.

Nature's rhythm, a heartbeat bright,
In the silence, there's pure delight,
Waves of regeneration softly weave,
Underneath all, we truly believe.

As the ocean cradles what has been tossed,
We find our strength in the paths we cross,
For every wave holds a tale anew,
In the undertow, our dreams break through.

Flotsam of Myth upon Ashen Seas

Upon the shores of the ashen grey,
The flotsam of myth tumbles and plays,
Stories drift on the breath of wind,
As echoes of legends begin to rescind.

Woven in whispers, tales intertwine,
Love and loss through the sea's design,
The horizon calls with a siren's tune,
In the shadows of night, beneath the moon.

With every wave, a memory cast,
Fragments of futures and echoes of past,
In the currents that swirl, truths collide,
Flotsam of myth, where we confide.

On journeys through waters both deep and wide,
We navigate dreams on an endless tide,
With hearts as sails, we embrace the sea,
In ashen seas, we find what will be.

For within the chaos of waves that churn,
The essence of stories begins to burn,
Flotsam gathers where the wild winds roam,
In every heart, the sea will feel like home.

Reflections on a Flickering Stream

A gentle breeze whispers dreams,
Where sunlight dances on the seams.
Ripples echo stories untold,
In the heart of nature, brave and bold.

Each stone bears witness to time's embrace,
Carving deep valleys in a tender grace.
The flickering light, a transient guide,
Lends a spark to the waters, flowing wide.

Beneath the surface, whispers awake,
Mirrors of secrets that ripples break.
Nature hums softly, a tune so sweet,
Where earth and sky in harmony meet.

In twilight's embrace, shadows arise,
Glistening droplets like stars in disguise.
As the sun dips low, colors collide,
A symphony whispered where dreams abide.

So let us wander where reflections gleam,
In the flickering world of a flowing stream.
For in each ripple, a story will bloom,
And in every glance, find the heart's room.

Elysian Views of Fading Light

As daylight dwindles, colors blend,
Whispers of magic in shadows send.
The horizon blushes, a soft farewell,
Where day and night share a secret spell.

Fields of gold tipped with crimson hue,
Breathe the last warmth as the night breaks through.
Stars flicker softly, a distant cheer,
Guiding lost wanderers who draw near.

In twilight's hush, the world slows down,
Wrapped in a velvet, nightwoven gown.
Elysian views unfold their charms,
Inviting the weary into their arms.

Silhouettes dance in the fading glow,
Stories awaken in whispers slow.
In the heart of dusk, dreams take flight,
Embraced by the mysteries of the night.

So linger awhile by the edge of fate,
Where twilight's wonders patiently wait.
For in these moments of gentle grace,
Life's fleeting beauty finds its place.

Fluttering Hearts Amidst Timbers

In the depths of the forest, love takes wing,
Where whispers of wonder and wildness cling.
Each step a heartbeat, soft and sweet,
Among ancient branches, where shadows meet.

Light filters gently through leaves up high,
Casting bright patterns, a painter's sky.
Rustles of leaves answer lovers' sighs,
In the heart of the wood, where true magic lies.

With fluttering hearts and eyes aglow,
We surrender to nature's radiant flow.
Time dances lightly on a delicate breeze,
Among towering timbers, under tall trees.

Soft as a whisper, the moments unfold,
Entwining two souls in the treasure they hold.
The symphony plays as twilight descends,
Forever united, where the forest bends.

Together we wander, a sanctuary divine,
Through fluttering leaves, with your hand in mine.
In the embrace of the woods, our love shall soar,
Where hearts find forever, forevermore.

The Enduring Dance of Fire and Water

In twilight's glow, a dance begins,
Where fire flickers and water spins.
Crackling warmth against the cool,
A timeless waltz, nature's jewel.

Flames leap high, a spirited song,
The river hums with notes so strong.
In harmony they swirl and play,
Creating magic at the end of day.

With splashes bright and sparks that soar,
A union crafted from ancient lore.
In every flicker, in every wave,
Memory's essence becomes the brave.

The moon reflects upon the tide,
As passion courses, side by side.
Embers fade, yet water flows,
An endless cycle, love that grows.

So let us witness this radiant dance,
Of fire and water in a timeless trance.
For in their embrace, eternity waits,
A journey of wonder that love creates.

Whispers of the Embered Waters

In shadowed glades where twilight sleeps,
The waters murmur secrets deep,
With glimmers of a flame's soft glow,
They dance like dreams, in ebb and flow.

Beneath the arch of ancient trees,
Whispers pass on gentle breeze,
Each ripple holds a tale untold,
Of brave hearts lost and legends bold.

The moonlight mingles with the tide,
As fireflies in the dark confide,
Their flickered light, a legacy,
Of hope that wanders, wild and free.

In currents swift, the memories swirl,
Of laughter shared in a hidden whirl,
Where echoes through the night sky weave,
A tapestry that we believe.

So linger near the embered shore,
Where time stands still, forevermore,
Let whispers guide your heart's intent,
And find the dreams that time has lent.

Echoes of the Fiery Nest

In caverns deep where shadows play,
The fiery nest, a bright display,
With glowing embers casting light,
Inviting all to share their plight.

The chirps of life, both near and far,
A symphony beneath the star,
Each echoing in rhythm proud,
A serenade unto the crowd.

Around the flame, the spirits dance,
With fervent hearts in fervent trance,
Their stories twine in orange hues,
Of every dream they dare to choose.

As feathers fall in ash anew,
From warmth of flame, the skies turn blue,
The whispers rise as daylight breaks,
In fiery nests, the magic wakes.

So gather 'round this sacred flame,
Where every heart ignites the same,
In echoes bold, let passions rise,
And soar anew towards the skies.

Beneath the Ashen Sky

Beneath the sky of muted gray,
Where whispers of the past still sway,
The ashes dance in silent flight,
While shadows wane to greet the night.

With embers low, the stories fade,
Of battles fought and fortunes made,
Yet in the dark, the sparks still gleam,
Carving the edges of our dream.

In every breath, a memory stirs,
Of hopes long lost, yet still occurs,
A tapestry of life and loss,
As shadows tread the line across.

The winds may carry tales of old,
Of hearts that dared, so brave and bold,
Yet amid the gray, there lies a spark,
To guide the wanderers from the dark.

So lift your gaze to ashen sky,
And search for wings that dare to fly,
For in the gloom, the light is near,
With every whisper, love is clear.

Resurgence of the Celestial Drift

In starlit nights where dreams arise,
The cosmic dance, a grand surprise,
With silken threads of fate entwined,
The universe, a map defined.

When currents sweep through open plains,
The whispers of the past remain,
A journey starts with every beat,
As hearts align in rhythmic heat.

Across the sky, the comets blaze,
In fleeting moments, time's embrace,
Reminding all of skies once bright,
That even dark gives way to light.

Through every drift, we find anew,
The echoes of what once we knew,
With every breath, a chance to soar,
To join the stars forevermore.

So let the cosmos guide your way,
With each resurgence, night and day,
Embrace the drift, and take your flight,
For in the stars, our dreams ignite.

www.ingramcontent.com/pod-product-compliance
Lightning Source LLC
Chambersburg PA
CBHW060633160125
20423CB00039B/887